CHILDREN'S STORYTELLERS

R.L. Stine

by Chris Bowman

BLASTOFF! READERS 4

BELLWETHER MEDIA • MINNEAPOLIS, MN

Note to Librarians, Teachers, and Parents:

Blastoff! Readers are carefully developed by literacy experts and combine standards-based content with developmentally appropriate text.

Level 1 provides the most support through repetition of high-frequency words, light text, predictable sentence patterns, and strong visual support.

Level 2 offers early readers a bit more challenge through varied simple sentences, increased text load, and less repetition of high-frequency words.

Level 3 advances early-fluent readers toward fluency through increased text and concept load, less reliance on visuals, longer sentences, and more literary language.

Level 4 builds reading stamina by providing more text per page, increased use of punctuation, greater variation in sentence patterns, and increasingly challenging vocabulary.

Level 5 encourages children to move from "learning to read" to "reading to learn" by providing even more text, varied writing styles, and less familiar topics.

Whichever book is right for your reader, Blastoff! Readers are the perfect books to build confidence and encourage a love of reading that will last a lifetime!

This edition first published in 2017 by Bellwether Media, Inc.

No part of this publication may be reproduced in whole or in part without written permission of the publisher. For information regarding permission, write to Bellwether Media, Inc., Attention: Permissions Department, 5357 Penn Avenue South, Minneapolis, MN 55419.

Library of Congress Cataloging-in-Publication Data

Names: Bowman, Chris, 1990- author.
Title: R.L. Stine / by Chris Bowman.
Description: Minneapolis, MN : Bellwether Media, Inc., 2017. | Series: Blastoff! Readers: Children's Storytellers |
    Includes bibliographical references and index.
Identifiers: LCCN 2016032042 (print) | LCCN 2016042452 (ebook) | ISBN 9781626175525
    (hardcover : alk. paper) | ISBN 9781681032993 (ebook)
Subjects: LCSH: Stine, R. L.–Juvenile literature. | Authors, American–20th century–Biography–Juvenile literature. |
    Children's stories–Authorship–Juvenile literature.
Classification: LCC PS3569.T4837 Z56 2017 (print) | LCC PS3569.T4837 (ebook) | DDC 813/.54 [B] –dc23
LC record available at https://lccn.loc.gov/2016032042

Editor: Christina Leaf   Designer: Steve Porter

Printed in the United States of America, North Mankato, MN.

Table of Contents

Who Is R.L. Stine?

R.L. Stine is the **pen name** of author Bob Stine. He created wildly popular horror **series** such as Goosebumps and Fear Street. His books are famous for twisting plots and **cliff-hanger** endings.

Bob is one of the best-selling children's authors ever. His books have been **published** in 32 languages. They have sold more than 400 million copies!

Bob Stine was born on October 8, 1943, in Columbus, Ohio. He grew up with two younger siblings, Bill and Pam.

Columbus, Ohio

N
W **E**
S

"My brother and I went to every scary movie. We didn't get scared. We always laughed!"
R.L. Stine

It Came from Beneath the Sea

! fun fact

Some of Bob's favorite films are *It Came from Beneath the Sea* and *Night of the Living Dead*.

Growing up, Bob and Bill liked to watch horror movies together. They also told each other scary stories before bed.

Bob did fine in school. However, he did not like to study. Instead, he listened to the radio and read comic books. His favorite comics were *Vault of Horror* and *Tales from the Crypt*.

At about age 9, Bob found an old typewriter in his attic. He used it to make his own comics and magazines. His friends passed them around at school.

fun fact

Bob's first magazine was called *The All New Bob Stine Giggle Book*.

"If you want to be a writer, don't worry so much about writing. Read as much as you can."
R.L. Stine

In college, Bob studied English. He also worked on his school's humor magazine, *Sundial*. He was an editor there for three years.

! fun fact

Working on magazines taught Bob to write quickly. This is how he finishes several books per year.

Bob taught for one year after college. Then he moved to New York to work as a writer. At first, he wrote for a few magazines. He also found love and got married.

"[Goosebumps] was the first book series to appeal equally to boys and girls."
R.L. Stine

Then Bob got a job with a **publisher** called Scholastic. He wrote and edited articles there. His wife, Jane, worked with him.

In time, Bob's job included creating a funny magazine called *Bananas*. Soon after, he began writing joke books for kids. He used the name **Jovial** Bob Stine.

! fun fact

For a few years, Jane was Bob's boss at Scholastic. Now she is his editor!

A Scary Idea

Bob's joke books were popular. But then an editor asked him to write a young adult horror **novel**. The book, *Blind Date*, was a fast favorite!

"There's some kind of secret kids network out there. Just kids telling kids about it, and this thing grew everywhere."
R.L. Stine

! **fun fact**

Most authors think of a title after the book is written. Bob comes up with his titles first. Then he writes a story to match.

Bob wrote more horror stories. In 1989, he started the Fear Street series. For younger readers, he created the Goosebumps series in 1992. Readers loved these books!

Horror with a Twist

Bob writes his books to be both scary and funny. His main rule is that his readers must know the stories are **fantasy**. He does not want to truly frighten kids.

16

His characters are usually normal kids facing scary situations. Parents and other adults are often unhelpful. The kids' creativity and intelligence get them back to safety.

SELECTED WORKS

Fear Street (1989 – Present)

Goosebumps (1992 – Present)

The Nightmare Room (2000 – 2001)

Mostly Ghostly (2004 – 2006)

Rotten School (2005 – 2008)

R.L. STINE

Goosebumps

Keep your eye on the birdie!

THE CUCKOO CLOCK OF DOOM

SCHOLASTIC

! fun fact

One of Bob's favorite Goosebumps books is *The Cuckoo Clock of Doom*.

Much of Bob's success comes from writing for many different readers. He writes from the **perspectives** of both boys and girls.

His books are not meant to teach morals. Bob just wants reading to be fun. He uses his books to **inspire** kids to read. Boys and girls who otherwise might not read often like his stories.

POP CULTURE CONNECTION

In 2015, *Goosebumps* came out in theaters. Actor Jack Black played R.L. in the movie. The film included monsters from many books in the series!

"In fact, [Goosebumps] were originally done for a girl audience. And then the fan mail started coming in, and it was half from boys."
R.L. Stine

Still Giving Goosebumps

So far, Bob has written more than 350 books in his nearly 40-year **career**. His stories have given millions of kids the creeps.

"Seriously, there are no morals. The moral is, RUN!"
R.L. Stine

IMPORTANT DATES

1943: Bob Stine is born on October 8.

1975: Scholastic starts printing Bob's magazine, *Bananas.*

1978: Bob's first book, *How to Be Funny*, comes out.

1986: *Blind Date* becomes Bob's first horror novel to be printed.

1989: *The New Girl* is the first book in Bob's Fear Street series.

1992: The first Goosebumps book, *Welcome to Dead House*, comes out.

2003: Goosebumps is named the world's best-selling book series of all time by Guinness Book of World Records.

2011: Bob receives the International Thriller Writers ThrillerMaster Award for his work in the thriller genre.

2014: The Horror Writers Association presents Bob with the Lifetime Achievement Award.

APPLE PAPERBACKS

HOW TO BE FUNNY

An Extra-Silly Guidebook
by Jovial Bob Stine

Bob regularly writes several books per year. New books in the Goosebumps and Fear Street series are still popular. Bob continues to give readers scary and funny stories to enjoy!

Glossary

career—a job someone does for a long time

cliff-hanger—a story or situation that is very exciting because what will happen next is unknown

fantasy—a story set in an unreal world often with superhuman characters and monsters

inspire—to give someone an idea about what to do or create

jovial—cheerful and friendly

novel—a longer written story, usually about made-up characters and events

pen name—a name used by a writer instead of the writer's real name

perspectives—points of view

published—printed someone's work for a public audience

publisher—a company that makes and prints books

series—a number of things that are connected in a certain order

To Learn More

AT THE LIBRARY

Purslow, Neil. *R.L. Stine*. New York, N.Y.: AV2 by Weigl, 2014.

Stine, R.L. *It Came from Ohio!: My Life as a Writer*. New York, N.Y.: Scholastic, 2015.

Stine, R.L. *The Cuckoo Clock of Doom*. New York, N.Y.: Scholastic, 1995.

ON THE WEB

Learning more about R.L. Stine is as easy as 1, 2, 3.

1. Go to www.factsurfer.com.

2. Enter "R.L. Stine" into the search box.

3. Click the "Surf" button and you will see a list of related web sites.

With factsurfer.com, finding more information is just a click away.

Index